Managing
Conflict

The Lessons Learned Series

Wondering how the most accomplished leaders from around the globe have tackled their toughest challenges? Now you can find out—with Lessons Learned. Concise and engaging, each volume in this new series offers twelve to fourteen insightful essays by top leaders in business, the public sector, and academia on the most pressing issues they've faced.

A crucial resource for today's busy executive, Lessons Learned gives you instant access to the wisdom and expertise of the world's most talented leaders.

Other books in the series:

Leading by Example
Managing Change
Managing Your Career

Managing Conflict

LES50NS

Copyright 2007 Fifty Lessons Limited
All rights reserved

Printed in the United States of America
11 10 09 08 07 5 4 3 2 1

Cataloging-in-Publication data for this title is
forthcoming.

⊰ A NOTE FROM THE ⊱
PUBLISHER

In partnership with Fifty Lessons, a leading
provider of digital media content, Harvard
Business School Press is pleased to an-
nounce the launch of Lessons Learned, a
new book series that showcases the trusted
voices of the world's most experienced
leaders. Through the power of personal
storytelling, each book in this series pres-
ents the accumulated wisdom of some of the
world's best-known experts and offers insights into how these individuals think, approach new challenges, and use hard-won
lessons from experience to shape their leadership philosophies. Organized thematically
according to the topics at the top of managers' agendas—leadership, change management, entrepreneurship, innovation, and
strategy, to name a few—each book draws
from Fifty Lessons' extensive video library
of interviews with CEOs and other thought

A Note from the Publisher

leaders. Here, the world's leading senior executives, academics, and business thinkers speak directly and candidly about their triumphs and defeats. Taken together, these powerful stories offer the advice you'll need to take on tomorrow's challenges.

We invite you to join the conversation now. You'll find both new ways of looking at the world, and the tried-and-true advice you need to illuminate the path forward.

⊰ CONTENTS ⊱

Contents

Managing Conflict

Putting Business Interests Above Personalities

Sir Peter Middleton

Former Chairman, Barclays Group

I HAVE ALWAYS found that the big things that cause organizations to get into difficulties have more to do with personalities than policies. The sort of difficulties I'm talking about are the ones where senior management falls out and the place gets into disarray—even if the fundamentals of the business are perfectly fine.

I'll give you two examples of that. When I was in the Treasury, there was a long-publicized and very well-known dispute between Margaret Thatcher and Nigel Lawson. As the Permanent Secretary of the Treasury at the time, it was extremely difficult to know quite what this dispute was about. It's a bit like having some sort of disease: you know what the symptoms are, but you're not very sure what the cause is. So, at a superficial level, it was quite obvious what they were arguing about, but in a fundamental sense it wasn't. It had much more to do with personalities—who was responsible for what—than it was about policies. The concern I had with that wasn't about their individual dispute but how we were going to keep the business of running the economy operating efficiently.

Somewhat to my astonishment, an almost similar thing happened in Barclays when I was halfway through my spell there. The chief executive suddenly resigned, and the

chairman followed him shortly thereafter.
Now, this was a dispute that was not at all
about policy—at least it wasn't so far as I
could discover—or about the way the business was being run. It was about two sorts of
different personalities. It wasn't really a dispute even, it was about mutual support—
whether they respected each other, whether
they got on—and it caused a serious crisis at
Barclays. Obviously, if you're a shareholder
and the management looks as if they've no
idea what they're doing, it's not a great incentive to hold the shares. So two very critical situations arose, as I say, not because of
fundamental policy—though there were
some policy issues—but from personalities.

Now, the question is: what do you do
about it? What you are trying to do is get the
business to take precedence over personalities; and provided there's agreement on the
business model or the government model or
whatever it is, I think it's a job that can be
done. But, it does require a sort of elder
statesman-type person to do it. You basically get people together, tell them to grow

up, and that if they don't work together they have to go—quite a difficult thing to do if one of them is the Prime Minister and one is the Chancellor, mind you—and that will quite often work.

If you tell people they're acting like children, they stop doing it. If it won't work, you really do have to act decisively and do something about it, because you cannot work in an organization that's at war. If I were to sum it up, I would say that first, you must be very aware that personalities are seriously important; they're more important the bigger the business, and they're more important the more senior people get.

Second, I'd say that personalities can be dealt with, but if they can't, you have to get rid of one of them.

TAKEAWAYS

- Organizations get into trouble when personalities get in the way of the business interests. The higher you go up the corporate ladder, the more important personalities and egos become, increasing the risk of disputes.

- Conflicts of personalities at a senior level will have a negative impact on the company's reputation with shareholders and inevitably on the company itself.

- Lead by example: do not allow your personal views to infringe on business interests.

Managing Conflict

✠ Keep a check on the personalities
within your business by getting to
know your staff. Curb any negativity
and conflicts of personality before
they happen.

Incentivizing Conflict

Mark Gerzon

Founder and President, Mediators Foundation

IN THE LATE 1990s, the House of Representatives had come to a grinding halt. The Democrats and Republicans were not working well together. They were sitting on the House floor looking at each other, and throwing up their hands and saying, "How can we even conduct business here? We're always in conflict, in static hostile conflict."

Managing Conflict

That's when they decided to have a retreat. I was asked because of my own work as a mediator and facilitator to be designer and facilitator of the first Bipartisan Congressional Retreats.

[This was] the first Bipartisan Congressional Retreat that the Democrats and Republicans went off for, a retreat to really say, "How can we rebuild a relationship between the two parties?" For me it was a very powerful experience of realizing these men and women whom we elected as our representatives—and who are skillful leaders, very thoughtful people from the private sector and public sector, caring people—were behaving like jerks.

And I looked at why. Why was Congress failing to be able to conduct the people's business? I realized there was an incentive structure that had been built into the House of Representatives, one in which nobody cared about the House; they only cared about their party. And if you create an incentive structure that rewards Democrats for acting like partisan Democrats and you create an incentive structure that gets Republicans to act like partisan Republicans, you're going to get a divided House; [the representatives] can't work with each other.

There was only an incentive structure for people to think about the victory for the Democrats or the Republicans. It was as if, in your company, you divided your company into two teams—the red team and the blue team—and said, "You're going to fight against each other for your jobs." It would create havoc and chaos inside a company. Well that's what it was doing inside the House of Representatives. And the result of the retreat that I was proud of was: for the first time, there were genuine friendships between Democrats and Republicans, where they developed a language for talking about the relationship between the two parties and why that relationship was key to the functioning of the House of Representatives.

Obviously, the House of Representatives is still a partisan place—the partisanship never went away and never will go away. But I think there was an awareness that was born:

democracy depends on something other than partisanship; it also depends on seeking common ground.

Inside a company, you have to look at the incentive structure you set up. Sometimes managers and CEOs will set up competitive structures, where you're actually getting people to compete against each other. If you do that, you have to be very careful that it's competition in the interest of the whole company.

I've been in company after company where if you, for example, reward incentives to sell your brand, you're going to get a brand-driven company with people caring only about their brand and not the company as a whole. You're going to get division fighting against division, and one sales force fighting against another sales force—if your incentives are about rewarding that narrow behavior, rather than rewarding the overall good of the company.

Be very careful how you create an incentive structure in your company, because that incentive structure will determine what kind of behavior you get. If you incentivize internal competition, you'll get internal competition; if you incentivize synergy, you'll get synergy.

The lesson for me from the work that I did with the U.S. Congress is that if you create rewards [for people] to behave like separate competing teams, you'll get separate competing teams. If you create rewards for people to work in the best interest of the company, you'll get people who work in the best interest of the company. And I find the bigger a company gets, the more critical that difference is, because ultimately you want synergy between these parts. I see too many companies where there is no synergy. Everybody's out for their own quarterly returns, making their division look good. And that doesn't add up to synergy for a company; that adds up to fragmentation and internal competition.

TAKEAWAYS

- ⚏ When an incentive structure is built into an organization so that individual parties or departments focus on their own interests, it is impossible to avoid conflict.

- ⚏ Individual groups need to find a common ground and work toward the best interests of the organization.

- ⚏ Set up incentive structures that encourage creativity and synergy, and find ways for disparate groups to work together.

- ⚏ Review current departmental or organizational incentive structures and revise them as needed to limit internal competition.

Keeping Peace Between People

Sir Mark Weinberg

Cofounder and President, St. James's Place Capital

AN IMPORTANT THING to recognize is that marketing and production or administrative people—in my case administrative people—are very different. They virtually come from different planets. The one lot is optimistic and extroverted. The other—the administrative/production people—is disciplined, somewhat pessimistic, and always sees the problems, which the marketing people don't. This makes it very difficult for them to work together.

They are always blaming each other for the fact that things are going slowly or not working out. This was a lesson I learned at my first company, Abbey Life, about thirty years ago. At that time I had a really first-rate marketing director and a first-rate administrative director, and the company did very well as a result. But each of them spent a lot of time coming to me to complain about the other one, because things always go wrong in business, however good your administration is. Things do go wrong, however good your marketing is. There will be times when you're overoptimistic or when the flow doesn't come through or when the salesman is unreasonable in his expectations from the administration.

The administrative director and the marketing director were separately coming to my office complaining about the other one and saying, "We have a very good marketing organization, but the administration is ruining the business and it's all the administrative director's fault." And so on. I used to hear a long story.

So, once a month I would call the two of them into my office. They would sit down, usually not feeling very comfortable with each other, and I would talk to both. I would say to the administrative director, "You are a first-rate administrative director. I think you're one of the best people; you run it very efficiently," and I would relate some of the good things that he'd done. Then I would look to the marketing director and say how incredibly well he's doing, what a good show he's doing, how well he's doing relative to the competition, and so on. They would both start nodding, and then I would say, "What we can't afford is friction between the marketing side and the administrative side because you have to work as a team; that's the only way we are going to work." They would start protesting that they hadn't been complaining about the other one and go off arm-in-arm as if they were the greatest of colleagues. I would close the door, take out my diary, and put down a date one month in the future to repeat the whole exercise, because it was going to happen again.

You don't change the beast, but I think you've got to keep peace between people and let them see each other's strengths so that they will work together.

TAKEAWAYS

- ⊰ Leaders must keep the peace when conflicts exist among key members of staff.

- ⊰ Maintain control of office politics and staff conflict by keeping communication lines open and regularly reviewing the situation.

Managing Conflict

⚜ Tackle staff conflicts or office politics head-on as soon as the situation occurs by calling a meeting with everyone involved. Work through what triggered the situation, stay positive, and encourage a resolution before the end of the meeting.

⚜ Provide positive feedback as often as possible. Do not just direct positive feedback to a specific person: ensure people are informed of the strengths of other colleagues, too.

Cohesive Management Resolves Disputes

Gary Wilson

Chairman, Northwest Airlines

BUSINESS IS A team sport, and you must have enormous teamwork to be successful. You must have a board that operates well as a team. You must have a CEO and a management team that operate with the board as a team, and you must have a management team that, in its own right, operates as a team. This means that the CEO is respected by his reports, the CEO respects his reports, and there is a very collegial environment.

At the companies where I've worked, I can't remember a time when we were with rational people who were looking at the numbers and the strategy where we didn't reach a unanimous decision. The decision just became obvious after we'd been through the pluses and minuses.

When my group bought Northwest Airlines in a leveraged buyout in 1989, our prime partner in doing this was KLM, which at that time was a relatively small European airline. Their vision was to participate in the American market because that was the only way they were going to be able to prosper in a world where the American market was half of the world market.

Peter Bough, who was the CEO and head of the management committee, had a vision to do something in the American market. His strategic objective was concurrent with our objective to buy Northwest Airlines, so

Managing Conflict

KLM provided much of the financing that was required to buy Northwest.

What KLM wanted in return was, basically, a very close alliance with the airline. In the early '90s, we lobbied very strongly with the U.S. government and with KLM to provide the first open-skies arrangement between the United States and a European country. The U.S. government approved this arrangement; we had our arrangement all worked out. Then the first Gulf War occurred, and Northwest had some financial problems, which we finally worked out in the summer of 1993. In our view, Mr. Bough, who had a big equity piece in the company, had questioned the motivation of both our ownership group and our management team, and he tried very hard to take control of the company.

As a result of his actions, we fought him legally from 1993—I think I have my dates right—to 1997. It cost a lot of legal fees, but most importantly, from a transatlantic point of view, there was a hiatus in the strategy of putting the two airlines together.

Managing Conflict

In 1997, because of our arguing continually with their supervisory board and because Mr. Bough wasn't doing well in other areas, the supervisory board terminated him. Leo van Wijk, who was his number two, took over as CEO.

Mr. van Wijk had been involved right from the start with Northwest. We all liked him a great deal and worked very well with him. In 1997, when this arrangement occurred, the companies immediately started to work more closely together. We actually negotiated a joint-venture agreement where the North Atlantic business of both parties was put into one joint venture, and it's been a profitable part of our business ever since.

Mr. van Wijk came on our board as a director, at our request, and I joined the board of KLM. There was no contractual arrangement for this, so it was a type of international diplomacy. The relationship has prospered because the management team had to truly be a team.

Business is not emotional. Business is business. You're working for the shareholder, and the shareholder doesn't really care whether the CEO of one company likes the CEO of the other company. Shareholders just want companies to be prosperous.

In my view, the lessons here are that you have to have a management team that is cohesive and that you can't have one person who dictates everything.

***

TAKEAWAYS

- ⚐ Because business so often works like a team sport, teamwork—among the CEO, management team, and board members—is imperative to success.

- ⚐ In business, everyone's job is to work for the shareholder, and that shareholder has only one concern: that the business be profitable.

Managing Conflict

⚔ Put aside personal feelings and auto-
cratic views, and team up with other
leaders to work in the best interests of
the shareholders.

⚔ Without teamwork, the business's
strategy and growth will be impeded.
To ensure future success, make teamwork a priority.

Dealing with Negative Behavior in the Workplace

Julia Cleverdon

Chief Executive, Business in the Community

IN THE EARLY DAYS, there were very few women coming through organizations. It's better now, but it still has a way to go in some places.

Managing Conflict

Somebody asked me if there was a lesson that I'd learned as a woman, and I suppose what I've learned is that you remember when people make put-down remarks to you.

The worst that will remain burned into my brain forever was back in British Leyland when I had been doing some work on absenteeism and sickness. I'd been analyzing whether people were sicker in the tool room than the plant shop or the pressing room, and whether there was anything that could help management do something to reduce the 30 percent absenteeism rate. With pool labor, you never knew who was coming in so you never had any stable teams. You simply sent people to whichever team was shortest at that moment, so it was having an appalling effect on the business.

I'd done quite a lot of work, being interested in it. And I'd say that, in the end, it's most important to measure absenteeism sickness by the name of the leader. They'll be sicker in tool room one under Brown than they are in assembly room two, under Smith. If you swap those supervisors, the lot that were well get sick and the lot that were sick get well. Leadership is the key to the commitment of people.

I'd written a report for my boss, a character called Mr. Russell Hooper. I'd prepared it, worked quite hard on it, and sent it to him. I hadn't been told to send it to anyone else. Then I was called to go to the big plant managers' meeting with the plant manager, a Mr. Tillston.

All of us were gathered around the plant. I was only representing the night shift to the industrial relations team, and I wasn't meant to speak; I was just meant to be taking notes. But [Mr. Tillston] asked an interrogative question to the whole room about absenteeism and sickness. Because I'd gotten rather enthusiastic about it, without thinking as to whether I was meant to be saying anything or not, I said, "Mr. Tillston, I've just done a big analysis on this. I think what we should be doing is analyzing absenteeism and sickness by the name of the supervisor rather than by shifts, which is the way we do it at the moment."

Managing Conflict

He said, "Well, well, well," looking down the line at this enormous plant managers' meeting. "Who is that speaking at the end? Ooh, it's a graduate! In fact, it's our Green Shield—stamping graduate, clutching her books of Green Shield stamps. Thinks she doesn't have to work as hard as everybody else. And it's a woman! Well, any more bright ideas, girlie?" At that moment, I just about managed not to burst into tears and said, "No, Mr. Tillston. Not at the moment."

My experience has been not to burst into tears, not to show that you're fazed in any way, and to hold your temper and your tongue. But always to be clear that if they make remarks like that, there's something about you that frightens them.

The most important thing that a senior manager can do is to acknowledge inside the organization that these things happen, and if they do happen, people need to know that they do not defend that sort of behavior.

One of the things it is important for senior people to do is to seek out opportunities to explain cogently and clearly their views about that area of life, and what behavior is acceptable in the workplace. You won't always—and couldn't possibly—eradicate everything; that's part of life's tapestry and problems. But you can make it very plain that you do not condone that behavior.

I think all one can do at the most senior level is to be very clear that, if information comes back to you or you pick up that what is going on is not [acceptable], the leadership line is that we do not want those values in our business.

TAKEAWAYS

- When people are taunted, it is often because their aggressor is frightened by them in some way.

- While senior managers need to be realistic in acknowledging that negative behavior exists, they must make it absolutely clear that they neither condone it nor regard it as acceptable in the workplace.

- ⚘ Have a "Say No to Negative Behavior" day throughout the organization to raise awareness of this problem. Make sure each department gets involved and use the event as an opportunity to push home the message that such behavior is not tolerated.

The "No Asshole" Rule

Robert Sutton

Professor of Management Science and Engineering,
Stanford University

THIS LESSON IS about one of the most obvious ideas that I've ever had, and it's certainly not my idea, yet is the one that has had the biggest effect on other people, at least in terms of the reaction. Where the story starts is when I was about eight years old, when my father, who was an entrepreneur, told me that he did everything in his life to avoid working with people who were assholes and, when he [got] involved with them, to avoid them at all costs.

So, this is one of the oldest ideas that I've ever heard of. And, fast-forwarding, I've always been interested in this notion of the "no asshole" rule. When I was a young assistant professor, we had this amazing faculty meeting where we were trying to decide which faculty members to hire. There was one guy who was extremely accomplished but was known as a jerk. A member of my department, I believe his name was Bob Carlson, said, "I don't care if this guy won the Nobel Prize, I don't want to have any assholes here; it'll ruin our department."

So that was floating around in my mind for a few years, and every now and then, when I was working with a start-up or another company, I'd hear this notion that we should do all that we can to avoid hiring assholes in this organization—and even a few of them would put it down as a rule. I forgot about it, and then I got a call from a woman named Julia Kirby, who said, "Do you have any ideas for a little essay for the *Harvard Business Review*?"

So, I wrote this little essay on the "no asshole" rule. And actually, the way I wrote her the note initially was, "I want to write an essay on something called the "'no asshole'" rule, but you guys at *Harvard Business Review* are way too conservative to publish the word *asshole*." I wrote the essay, working with Julia, and it had the word *asshole* appear, I believe—I haven't gone back and counted it—eight or nine times. In fact, I put it in more times than I really wanted on the theory that they would cross it out all but maybe once, but then they left them all in.

To my amazement, the *Harvard Business Review* published this "No Asshole Rule" [article], which essentially said three things: one, you should avoid hiring assholes when you can; two, more importantly, you shouldn't allow people to get away with it; and three—it had a little creative twist at the end—that there was an argument that maybe you should have just one asshole in your organization, because there's literature on deviance that says that when you have one person who's the oddball, actually everybody else is better because they see how not to behave.

The whole of the trend of deviance is actually fairly fascinating. There's also related literature on littering. It actually turns out that people are less likely to litter into a setting that has one piece of garbage than none, because the norm violation, if you will, is clear. It's the same thing with any sort of behavior, so if there's one person in your office who's a total jerk, there's an argument that you might want to leave just that one person. The problem is when everybody becomes jerks.

The most amazing thing was the response to the article. I received three hundred or four hundred e-mails from all over the world, and I would usually respond to them because so many of them would be so heartfelt. People would ask, "What do I do?" And, in reality, I guess there were three sorts of strategies that I would recommend. The first one is: if you actually can have some way to bring together some political power, you might want to work to change the norms.

The second thing that I tell them is: you can always find a way to leave, if you can get another job, and you have to try. Or, if you're a manager you can actually use it as a criterion to fire people.

The third one is something that I don't think is talked about enough in organizational life management books. [If] you start reading, the message tends to be about passion and caring and devotion—it's like Jim Collins's "You're on the bus or you're off the bus." Everything is about the more you care, the better things are going to be. My argument is that actually, very often in life, there are times when learning not to care and learning to be indifferent is incredibly important—and it's something that we don't teach people enough. So, if you're in a situation where there's nothing you can do about changing it, you might as well just ignore it and go on and do what's best for you—maybe hide from your boss a little bit.

Managing Conflict

Indifference and not caring is something that I think we need to teach people to get better at. It's harder to do that in life, but one of my goals as an adult is to start getting better and better at figuring out what doesn't matter to me, and ignoring it.

TAKEAWAYS

- 🔖 The rule of avoiding working with, or hiring, jerks is adopted by many organizations to avoid disharmony in the workplace.

- 🔖 Don't allow staff to get away with antisocial or "oddball" behavior, as such behavior is likely to cause office conflict.

- 🔖 Adopt the "no asshole" rule when recruiting new staff by considering how existing colleagues will interact with the new recruit and whether they appear to have the personality traits, as well as the skills, you are seeking.

⊰ Put out some feelers to determine what recruits are really like. Take the time to find out who you are hiring before you bring them on board.

—◆◆◆—

Dealing with High-Maintenance Individuals

—◆◆◆—

Dawn Airey

Former Managing Director, Sky Networks, BSkyB

DEALING WITH high-maintenance
individuals is something that most leaders
will have to do at some time. I started
out at Channel 4 as controller of Arts

& Entertainment. I was plucked from relative obscurity, when I was responsible for Kids' & Daytime programming at ITV. The then-director of Programs, John Willis, said, "Let's have breakfast, Dawn."

Anybody who knows me knows I do not like getting up early in the morning, and the idea of a breakfast meeting is ghastly; I'd much rather stick pins in my eyes. John said, "Now, it could be to your advantage, so let's have breakfast together." And I thought, "I really don't want breakfast." And he said, "We'll breakfast at the Savoy." I thought, "Well, I've never had breakfast at the Savoy—Okay, I'll go to breakfast."

I was walking over the bridge, and then I realized the controller of Arts & Entertainment for Channel 4 had just gotten a job as managing director of Granada. I thought, "Oh bugger, that's what he's going to ask me about—that job." And it was. As it was, we got on extremely well. I was offered the job, and I took it.

Managing Conflict

And there was a degree of outrage. Television, for all of its liberal nature and approach to everything, is actually in some ways quite white-collar, middle-class male. It has changed very tangibly over the last five years, but I'm going back over ten years. From nowhere, the great cultural institution of Channel 4 had appointed somebody who didn't have great experience in arts and entertainment but had a good track record of being pretty commercial and shaking things up. I went to meet all of my senior creative people and controllers, and an individual who shall remain nameless came up to me after my first day, and said, "Well, I really don't like you, and actually, I really don't want you to be my boss. In fact, I don't think you're very good at all; in fact, I think you're a crock of shit."

I said, "Well, that is very interesting, and I really appreciate your candor because I'm going to be equally candid back. Which is to say that I know you are a very, very talented commissioning editor, but if the pain of working with you outweighs the gain—or in fact, even if the pain equals the gain— I will have you out of this door so bloody quickly—and don't think I won't, because I will. So I'm very happy to deal with you as a high-maintenance individual, but if that high maintenance is not equaled by over-delivery, you are out on your ear."

The interesting thing is that we had a very good relationship from then on because nobody had taken on this individual in such a candid way before and said, "Okay, that's fine, but I'm the boss, and this is the way it's going to be." And he responded actually rather well for it.

The lesson from that is: whenever you put together a group of people, it's a very interesting management challenge—you're always going to have those you feel closer to. There are always going to be some people who are a little bit crotchety, or they're always going to come at things in a slightly different way. Or if they can be irritating, they will be. But if you work with a group of people, you have to embrace those differences.

Managing Conflict

If somebody becomes out of kilter and really, really destructive within the team, or really negative for no reason other than they can and they've never been controlled before, you just have to deal with it head on, as quickly as possible. Make it very clear what the rules of engagement are, and make it very clear what the consequences are if they're breached. If the gain doesn't outweigh the pain, it's very simple: it's P-45 [pink slip] time.

TAKEAWAYS

◁ In the work environment, there will always be some individuals with whom you get along more than others. The trick is in knowing how to manage the difficult or high-maintenance individuals.

Managing Conflict

- ⚔ Challenging difficult individuals' behavior can either lead to a productive working relationship or cause them to leave the organization. As a leader, however, you must act; simply ignoring the situation is not a viable option.

- ⚔ Encourage those in your organization to understand the parameters of acceptable behavior through some light-hearted yet focused role-playing.

- ⚔ Tackle the issue of high-maintenance individuals as soon as the situation arises. Call them into a meeting and explain to them the company's rules of engagement.

Dealing with Bullying

Barbara Stocking

Director General, Oxfam GB

THE WORST CASE of bullying that I've ever experienced was when I was in the National Health Service. I started as Regional Director in 1993, and in the early years, there was a very supportive culture at the top. For example, that meant that people got things done by encouraging people

[and] motivating people, not by just simply trying to tell them what to do.

As the years went by, the culture at the top became much more macho. In part, it was after the Labour government came in, and it started setting much more strict and severe targets for the NHS. And the culture then became very much, "Tell the people what to do, don't put up with any nonsense, and make them get on with it." Now that was difficult for me and my style, in any case, because I really do believe that people will come with you if you can explain to them what needs to be done and why it's to be done—and especially in the NHS, where people are trying to do better in delivering service. But the culture did get tougher and harder.

I found that particularly difficult on the NHS executive board because I was the only woman regional director of eight, and that was throughout the whole time, the eight years I was a regional director in the NHS. The other woman on the board was the chief nursing officer. In the early years, again, that was not a problem for me. But as the culture got more and more macho, there was more bullying—bullying clearly down inside the organization with the chief executives of our trust and health authorities. Also, that was the tone much more on the NHS executive board.

My particular personal experience was that I used to chair the group of regional directors, where we got our ideas together about was happening, what could work, and what couldn't work. And some of the new regional directors who had been appointed didn't like it that a woman whom they thought was probably not tough enough was leading their little group. On a number of occasions, one or two of them caused me quite a lot of trouble in trying to chair those meetings and get to some resolution. I learned a lot then about how to handle bullying. First of all, of course, you have to talk to people about it, your friends and colleagues, and really try to understand whether you're doing the right thing—whether you need to change. You have to talk just a bit more about what's going on.

This particular incidence came to a head at one meeting over a very small issue. I was trying to arrange the next meeting, and because it was in the middle of August with the bank holidays, I said, "Can we meet then, or are you all going to be away on holiday?" The particular regional director said to me, "I don't know when I'm on holiday. My wife does that." And I said, "I think you're very lucky to have a wife." Which rather brought the house down.

That really taught me the lesson that if you can deal with bullies by, in a sense, not noticing their bullying but just actually dealing with humor about their outrageousness, then you can get a lot of good will on your side. And actually you reinforce your own self-esteem and self-confidence.

I think wherever you are in the organization, you have to do something similar. You have to get some personal support, and in a way you also have to try and handle [the situation] with as much self-confidence as you can. But clearly if you are more junior in the organization, it's really important that you do raise it up the line, either with your own manager or with somebody in human resources to really talk to them about what's happening.

Again, in the organizations where I've worked, I've tried to make the culture as open as possible, so that people know that if something is going on that they will be heard and taken very seriously, and that they may be able to speak to their own manager. But if they can't, there are other places they can, and they can bring it right up the line.

If you are seen volleying from the top of the organization or word gets to you that something is happening, it's very important indeed that you take action and you are seen to take action. What I mean by that is you have to be trusted to investigate an issue and to do that fairly and properly—because it may be something that's been raised that isn't true—but [you have to let people know] that that's going on and to make it clear.

Managing Conflict

I've seen that in Oxfam. There was a particular concern from South America, where staff wrote in to me and said they thought something was happening. We sent out an enquiry team, and the issue, as always, was rather more complex than it seemed, and there were faults on both sides. But what was known by all staff in the region was that an independent team had come in and made the inquiries, and I had responded to them and actually wrote back to staff saying what we were going to do.

So, it's very important from the top that if any suggestions of bullying or harassment or anything come up, you are really seen to handle them and handle them fairly.

———◆———

TAKEAWAYS

———◆———

- ⚑ The first step in handling bullying is to talk to colleagues about it, make it known, and decide on the path to take to correct the situation.

- ⚑ One way to deal with bullies is to disarm them. This can be accomplished at times by dealing with their bullying with humor.

- ⚑ Do some research on bullying: who bullies whom and when, and why bullying occurs. Then assess your workplace: are there things in the environment that make bullying more likely to occur? If so, take action to reduce those chances of it occurring.

⊰ Make bullying a serious offense.
While you will have to mete out discipline on an individual basis, determine the possible ranges of discipline
(from light to severe) to be meted out
once the case has been thoroughly
investigated.

The Art of
Self-Control

William Ury

Coauthor, Getting to Yes

ONE OF THE most challenging negotiations that I've been confronted with is a negotiation I had in the course of mediating between President Hugo Chavez in Venezuela and his political opposition. At a time in the early 2000s, numerous international observers were afraid that Venezuela was

going to tip into the kind of political violence that bedevils its neighbor Columbia.

Tensions were high. There were mass
demonstrations, some violence, and a coup
d'état reversed. It was a very tough situation.
At one point I had a nine o'clock appoint-
ment with the president at his palace. So I'm
waiting there—ten o'clock, eleven o'clock.
Finally at midnight, I'm ushered into the
president's office thinking I was going in for
a one-on-one, but I'm there with his entire
cabinet behind him.

I'd been speaking to some of his minis-
ters earlier and said so to Chavez. I congrat-
ulated him and said, "Mr. President, it
seems like things are improving a little between you and the political opposition. It
seems like we're making some progress."

He took that as a cue to say, "What do you
mean that we're making progress? Those
SOBs!" He really got into a fury. "And you
neutrals are being fooled blind; you're not
seeing what they're doing." I was sitting
there wondering, "What am I supposed to

do?" Because he's been attacked, I'm feeling personally attacked. That was the situation.

So, what I did—what I do in those situations—was just say to myself, "Hey, stay cool; stay steady; and remember why you're here." I realized that if I became defensive and started replying in kind, it wasn't going to serve my purpose; it wasn't going to advance the process. It wouldn't serve me in any way to get into a shouting match with the president.

So I waited, and I waited, and I didn't react. After an hour, suddenly, he calmed down. He turned to me and in a very resigned and somewhat exasperated voice said, "Ury, what should I do?"

That was my moment; I was ready. I had come with a proposal to say, "Hey, this is Christmas; let's have a cooling-off truce. Everyone, take some time out, relax, have a nice holiday, and get cool minds. Then we can focus on the problem."

At the end he was inviting me to go on a tour of Venezuela with him—very amicable.

Managing Conflict

What I learned from that is: one of the greatest powers in negotiation is the power of not reacting. Human beings are reaction machines. As Ambrose Bierce once said, "[Speak when you are] angry, [and] you will make the best speech you will ever regret."

We often do that, whether it's in the boardroom or at the office cooler. We lose it. And in negotiation in particular, where we're trying to advance our interests, the single biggest barrier isn't the other side; it turns out to be us. It's our own natural human reactions, which is why it's so important not to react.

I like to use a metaphor of going to the balcony. In other words, take a step back from the situation. Imagine you're negotiating on a stage, and part of your mind goes up to a mental balcony, someplace overlooking the stage, a place where you can get some perspective. You can see what's really going on; you can keep your eyes on the prize. Ask, "What are my real objectives in this negotiation?" Whether I'm negotiating with a tough client, or tough boss, or tough colleague, I ask, "What are my real objectives here, and how can I best advance them?"

Keep your eyes on the prize so you don't get mad. You don't get even, but you get what you want.

TAKEAWAYS

- When negotiating, especially when discussions are emotionally charged, the best strategy comes in not reacting.

- Focus on your own objectives and how you can best achieve them, and step back from the situation as needed to gain new perspective.

- The greatest obstacle is not the opposition; it is ourselves.

Stick to the Facts and Stand Your Ground

Neville Isdell

Chairman and CEO, The Coca-Cola Company

THERE'S AN OLD saying by a famous
Irish rugby captain—and that's a very different game: retaliate first. I don't think that's
the way to manage conflict. The way that you
manage conflict in a business situation is to
be fact-based.

Managing Conflict

If you don't have your facts right, then you're going to get into a situation of "them and us" or "me and you." Personalities get involved. Egos get involved. Positions are taken that are very difficult to move away from.

But if you are talking to the facts, and you're restricted to the facts, then I believe you are able to move a dialogue forward to a place where you both must have some sort of victory out of it, to a place where you can get a positive resolution that is good for both parties.

I'll give you a very early story. It's about managing conflict in different ways. But I'm not saying you're always the nice guy and that you don't take risks. This was in Zambia, during my first years in the business. I happened to be running all of the operations outside the plant. A truck was loading, cases crashed off, and glass was all over the place. Obviously, one of my people had made a mistake.

The general manager came out, and he started yelling at me and everyone else

around. I just took it and sat there. "Okay,
we'll fix it. That's fine." I then bit my lip
because the first thing I wanted to do, as
one always does, was resign and walk away.

I'm as human as the next guy. I get mad.
But I actually went into his office, and in a
very measured way, I said, "Mr.,"—and I
won't give you his name—"I don't mind if
you call me into this office and you yell
and scream at me for what happened outside. You have the perfect right to do that.
There's a mistake's that's been made, and
I'll take complete responsibility for it. But
please, never again, yell at me outside the
office; never do it in front of my people."

By the way, he was known for actually
going around yelling at people. His nick-
name was Mussolini. Do you know what?
He yelled at other people, but he never ever
again yelled at me in public. He did yell at
me in private, but he never, ever yelled at
me again in public.

So that's a lesson the other way around
about conflict, about how you manage conflict when you're on the receiving end and

how you can actually get someone who doesn't handle interpersonal relationships the right way—because he [the general manager] didn't—and actually get a win out of the situation for yourself.

Sometimes there isn't a solution. You'll have to bite your tongue and just wait because not everything is resolvable. But I believe that with fundamental integrity, fundamental honesty, and the proper use of facts, conflicts can be resolved really effectively, even with people who are extremely difficult and maybe overly demanding.

I haven't always succeeded in biting my tongue and waiting. I've also failed. I've also taken my tail, put it between my legs, and gone off and made a mistake. You learn from those. Of course, you learn more from your mistakes than you do from your successes. And I've made mistakes, too.

TAKEAWAYS

- ⚏ In negotiations, retaliation is not the way to manage conflict.

- ⚏ In predicaments where egos get involved, it's virtually impossible to move toward resolution.

- ⚏ No matter how forcefully the other side unleashes emotions, maintain composure and engage in fact-based negotiations.

- ⚏ Check your emotions at the door, and state your case clearly and factually. Only then can you be successful at negotiations.

Communicating Through Conflict

Roger Fisher

Coauthor, Getting to Yes

ONE OF MY students, Jamil Mahauad, became president of Ecuador, and I got to know him fairly well. [Ecuador and Peru] were at the edge of war. I talked with Mahauad, and I got him to invite President Fujimori of Peru to come talk with him.

Managing Conflict

[Fujimori] said, "But we're enemies. Why should I come and talk to you?" And Mahauad said, "I think it would be useful if you came and we talked together."

And so President Fujimori of Peru came to visit President Mahauad of Ecuador, and the two of them sat side by side. Then I had my student Mahauad ask Fujimori for his advice. And [Fujimori] said, "I should give you advice?"

[Mahauad said], "Yes we have this problem of getting along. We've been fighting wars. . . . Give me your ideas on what you think we ought to be doing."

[Fujimori] said, "You want my advice?"

And [Mahauad] said, "Yes, and I'll give you some of my advice."

The two of them sat there side by side, working together: Give me your ideas. How can we work together better? What can we do?

Imagine the picture of them on the front page of the paper, the two presidents, sitting next to each other talking to each other when they had previously been sending notes back and forth threatening war. Now they were seen talking together and trying to figure out how to go forward.

That changed it from a war situation into one of [talking about these issues and] saying, "Let's get together and talk about it, realize that it's not just arguing; I'm trying to give you advice on how you should deal with the situation.

"So I come and try to put myself in your shoes: How do you see it? How can I help you see it in a way that will be helpful to you, where you can go forward? I'm not telling you what to do; I'm not fighting with you." And much more.

"I have to get on your side, understand what you're thinking about it; what you're worried about—your concerns, your interests—and how I can help you deal with your side."

Negotiation is recognizing that it's not just the other side that has a problem but that we have a problem together. When you negotiate, you want to understand each other's perceptions. How do you see it?

How do I see it? How do we change it from adversarial to side by side, so that we're both working on this?

TAKEAWAYS

- Even the most adversarial of enemies can reach compromise by opening the lines of communication.

- Ask an opponent for advice and work to truly understand his or her concerns to effectively diffuse a potentially volatile situation.

- Recognize that the problem is not yours alone—or your opponent's. Instead it is a problem that you both share and that you must work together to solve.

Tough Conversations

Stephen Dando

Group HR Director, Reuters

IF YOU ARE espousing a certain approach in the organization, it is quite important that when people manifestly operate outside of that, that you find ways of saying something about it; calling it to account, if you like.

Easier said than done. I was leading the HR and organizational aspects of a major change program. This was a change program that affected quite a number of different countries and businesses within the total business. We were completely reengineering the processes that held those businesses together. It required a number of small business units to, in a sense, surrender some of their autonomy, their decision making and so on, for the greater good of the organization; and not all of them were particularly happy to do that.

The senior team that was responsible for this whole part of the organization was made up of the different bits. There were a lot of political behaviors going on among [the team members], who were fighting their own corners. When I look back on it now, it is quite clear that what we should have done, because we could see it happening, was embolden the chief executive and one or two other people to declare that there was something going on, and to deal with the behaviors rather than working around them.

If you experience someone who is clearly behaving in a way that is out of step with whatever it might be—the values, if you've got a declared set of values, or some other expectation about how people do things—it is very important to deal with that at an individual level, to find a way of noticing with that individual what's happening.

Find a way of talking about it. What is difficult about that for most people is that when you're confronting someone in that way, however sensitively, they will quite naturally be very defensive; so it is a difficult conversation to have. For that reason, in my experience, most people will duck that most of the time, because people will tend to argue and disagree with quite a lot of what's being said.

One of the things that you can do to make that a better conversation is to talk about it in terms of how it leaves you feeling, and what you're experiencing in terms of that person's behavior, rather than in the ways we often talk about these things.

If we generalize and talk about the impact he or she might be having for other people, or for the effectiveness of the organization or something, then it is very easy for that person to disagree. That's a perspective and that person may agree or disagree, but if one is willing to bring it back to one's personal experience, that's not something that you can disagree with. If I say to you, "Look, there's something about the way that you're dealing with something, talking to me, relating to me, whatever it might be; and here's the experience that that's having *for me* and here's how *I feel* about this. Whatever you might want to say, you can't really disagree with how I'm feeling." I think that can be quite effective.

TAKEAWAYS

⊰ People often become territorial and resistant to change when faced with massive upheaval, particularly if they believe it will lead to diminished responsibility.

⚏ Behaviors that go against company strategy must be dealt with directly, rather than worked around.

⚏ During a tough conversation people will often get defensive, so control the situation and maintain a level of calm by preparing your main points in advance.

⚏ To improve a difficult situation, discuss how the individual's behavior is making you feel.

If You're in a Fight, Make Sure You Win

Kay Koplovitz

Founder, USA Networks

IN 1992 I WAS running USA Networks and getting ready to launch the Sci-Fi Channel. Ted Turner was running WTBS, and he was getting ready to launch TNT. It was a particular year where many of the contracts for distribution were coming up for renewal, or new contracts were coming up for new networks, and so all of us were out there with the cable industry trying to get these contracts signed so we could continue the networks we had and bring new networks into their systems.

There was one operator who had about 1,600,000 cable subscribers at the time. He was one of the largest ten or twelve cable operators, and he decided—he was a big devotee of Ted Turner's—that he would cancel USA Networks and put on TNT in its place. The reason he gave was that the programming was too violent for his communities—and so he said in his letter of cancellation, which was stunning because no one had, at that point, ever cancelled all of their systems across the board. There is always some contentious activity, maybe a system would get dropped here and there, but not across the board.

So, it was a shot across the bow, to say the very least. He was trying to stampede other cable operators into doing the same thing—into dropping USA and putting TNT on in its place. I didn't know how strong a movement that was, or whether it was a movement or not, or if it was just Glen being Glen—Glen Jones. So, I had to take it extremely seriously.

We had contracts for carriage, and one of the things we had to do was look at was whether we could keep our contract intact. Could we enforce our contract and make him continue to carry us? Now, cable operators had the opportunity to cancel at certain points in their contract; they had a thirty-day window where if they wanted to cancel, they could; and he was in one of those periods. But we found out through the depositions—and it was actually the last deposition that we were taking—that one of the executives of Jones said, "Oh yeah, that's when we were told to backdate all the documents so that they were within the thirty-day time period."

And we said, "Could you explain that a little bit more to us, please?" He was told to backdate the cancellation document. Voilà. Bingo. We take that, we go to court, we make our argument, and, not to draw out the story, we won that argument. But in order to do that, we had taken our field forces out, and we were challenging [Jones's] franchises across the country. I took him into the most serious court; I brought in the fiercest lawyers I could bring in to fight my case. I decided that even though this was a client and I was risking distribution throughout the country, and possibly with other cable operators, I had to make that clause stick.

If [Jones's people] did not file [the documents] in a proper way, which we suspected they didn't, and in a timely fashion—because it came very late to us, and they said, "Oh, it must have gotten lost in the mail"—I had to make that [clause] stick to make the rest of my contracts valid with the other distributors. It was a very tense time. I had to make a lot of decisions about how to deploy and how to fight, and I fought on every level—at the local level, at the state level, and at the federal level. I fought him on every front because I was determined to win that battle.

Managing Conflict

But the lesson I learned is, if you're going to take on one of your valued customers, which you really don't want to do if you don't have to, then you better pull out all your guns and start firing them, because you're not playing a game anymore; now it's war. The good thing is, at the end of it, we won that case in court, our network had to be reinstated on all of [Jones's] systems, and he had to pay us top-rate card rates for ten years, so it was a sweet victory.

TAKEAWAYS

- ⚔ Effective leaders recognize when a battle becomes a war, even if it means taking on valued partners.

- ⚔ When leaders find themselves in all-out wars, they shouldn't hesitate to unleash every resource necessary to win those wars.

⊣ Identify the skills and tactics that are effective in diffusing conflict. Develop a plan for coaching these skills in your team or the organization's key stake-holders.

⊣ Task your team with identifying a battle and developing a strategy for winning that battle. Ask them to document the challenges, desired outcomes, and the resources and tactics necessary to win that battle.

Always
Avoid Conflict
If Possible

Robert Johnson

Founder, Black Entertainment Television

MANAGING CONFLICT is something
that a chief executive tries to avoid. You
never want to get into a situation where you
essentially call it conflict, because part of
being in business is wanting to have positive
relationships with any stakeholder you have.

Managing Conflict

I always look at relationships and think, "How can I build this relationship or build this opportunity to be in business where we never get into conflict?" I try to do that by putting myself in the shoes of the guys on the other side of the table. What is it they actually need from me? What is it they actually want to make this relationship work? I try my best to find those situations where it works.

Now, if it doesn't work that way, you have some options. Your options are to end the relationship or to yield a little bit more, as long as it doesn't hurt your basic objective. Or you can sit down and try to reason toward something that's going to be a little bit of compromise on both parts. That's my natural instinct.

I try to avoid conflict, and part of that comes from the fact that I'm a minority entrepreneur. It's very tough to go in and get into a conflict situation, because most of your vendors, your outside stakeholders, are white-owned companies. You get a reputation really quickly if you are too aggressive, and that hurts your growth pattern, because nine out of ten times, you're going to be dealing with a white company to get any kind of business. So you really want to avoid that.

But when I do have to do it, I do it in a way where I simply state my case clearly as to why I think the situation should change. I'll give you one example. I felt very strongly that the cable operators should give more distribution to BET than [it] had been given. I pointed out to them that African Americans are heavy cable subscribers; that African American entertainment is enjoyed by people of all colors and all ethnic groups; that some of the top recording artists and entertainers are African Americans; and that cable licenses are granted by communities that have, in many cases, African American elected officials. It just made sense to do it, in addition to giving opportunities for hiring African American employees, which is something this country believes in: equal opportunity. And you say it up front.

I remember one time calling cable operators a bunch of cable slumlords. Basically, they operate just like housing slumlords who charge high rent, don't fix up the dwelling, and let the people live in squalor. [Cable operators] charge African American consumers money to install the cable, but they don't deliver much content or black programming that would appeal to their viewing interests.

That [analogy] created an uproar in the cable industry. "Gee, Bob, why are you saying this about us? The people on Capitol Hill are going to hear this. The FCC is going to hear this."

My intent was clear. I wanted to send a message that I was not going to lie down and allow them to not respect BET as a product that their consumers wanted—consumers who were paying forty dollars a month. [In addition, cable operators disregarded the fact] that blacks, as a percentage of the population, subscribe to cable more than whites do.

So I made my case that cable operators couldn't take blacks for granted, and I said it publicly. That message resonated in two ways. Some people again realized, "You know, he's right. We have to do more to serve this market. They're good cable subscribers, and this guy's not going to be a pushover."

That example is what I call last-resort conflict. Most business people are successful. My feeling is they don't engage in warfare; they engage in negotiations. War is diplomacy by any other means. To me, if you're in a war, you've failed.

TAKEAWAYS

- Being in business means fostering positive relationships and avoiding conflict where possible.

- Build opportunities whereby leaders see situations from the other person's

point of view and make small compro-
mises as needed.

⚔ Where conflict is unavoidable, state
the case clearly. Doing so makes one a
stronger leader and heightens one's
ability to achieve objectives.

⚔ Avoid starting a war at all costs; instead,
engage in diplomatic negotiations.

⊰ ABOUT THE ⊱ CONTRIBUTORS

Dawn Airey is the former managing director of Sky Networks, the U.K.'s largest digital pay television provider. In May 2007 she was appointed the Director for Global Content at ITV Productions, one of Europe's leading production companies.

Ms. Airey has worked in television for twenty years. She joined Britain's Central TV as a management trainee in 1985 and became Channel 4 liaison officer a year later. In 1988 she was made Controller of Program Planning. The following year she became Director of Program Planning, with specific responsibilities for the schedule and its off- and on-screen promotion.

In January 1996 Ms. Airey was appointed Director of Programs for Channel 5 (now Five). She became CEO in October 2000—a position she held until the end of 2002. In January 2003 she joined British Sky Broadcasting, where she took on the newly created post of Managing Director, Sky Networks, until her departure 2007. Ms. Airey joined ITV Productions in May 2007.

Ms. Airey is also a director of easyJet.

About the Contributors

Julia Cleverdon is Chief Executive of Business in the Community, an organization dedicated to improving corporate impact on society.

Ms. Cleverdon started her career working in industrial relations at British Leyland. She was director of The Industrial Society's Education and Inner City Division from 1981 until 1988 before becoming CEO of Business in the Community—the movement of seven hundred companies across the United Kingdom committed to continually improving their positive impact on society—in 1992.

During her time there, one of her key roles has been to lead "Seeing Is Believing," the initiative launched in conjunction with HRH the Prince of Wales to help business leaders see the role business can play in tackling social problems. To date, more than fourteen hundred business leaders have taken part.

Ms. Cleverdon is also a director of InKind Direct, the charity that acts as a clearinghouse for surplus goods from the corporate sector that are channeled to good causes in the voluntary sector.

Stephen Dando is Group HR Director for Reuters, a global information company and the world's largest international multimedia news agency.

Mr. Dando began his career as a graduate trainee with Austin Rover in 1984 and since then has held a wide range of positions in Ferranti International, United Distillers, Diageo, UDV Europe, and, most recently, Guinness Ltd., where he was global Human Resources Director, prior to supporting the integration of Guinness and UDV.

About the Contributors

In June 2001 Mr. Dando joined the BBC as Director of Human Resources and Internal Communications. He became a member of the BBC's Executive Committee. Mr. Dando led the transformation of the BBC's human resources function, delivering significant improvements in effectiveness and annualized savings, which were achieved on target in March 2004. He implemented the BBC's largest-ever leadership training program in conjunction with Ashridge Business School, which won a World of Learning award in 2004. In January 2004 he became Director, BBC People, to reflect the new name of the BBC division he led.

He joined Reuters as its Group HR Director in April 2006.

Roger Fisher is Samuel Williston Professor of Law, Emeritus, at Harvard Law School and the coauthor of *Getting to Yes.*

Professor Fisher earned his AB from Harvard University and his LLB from Harvard Law School.

Before joining the Harvard Law School faculty, Professor Fisher worked for the U.S. government in Paris, practiced law in Washington, D.C., and served as an assistant to the Solicitor General in the Department of Justice.

In 1958 Professor Fisher was appointed lecturer on law, and in 1960 he became professor of law. He was appointed as Samuel Williston Professor of Law in 1976 before becoming director of the Harvard Negotiation Project in 1980, a position he still holds.

About the Contributors

In 1984 Professor Fisher founded the Conflict Management Group (CMG), an innovative leader in peace-building work and conflict resolution in troubled regions worldwide. CMG merged with Mercy Corps in 2004.

Professor Fisher is the coauthor of *Getting to Yes*, *Beyond Reason: Using Emotions as You Negotiate*, and numerous other publications.

Mark Gerzon is Founder and President of the Mediators Foundation, an organization that promotes education, addresses social issues, and fosters global understanding.

Mr. Gerzon studied at Harvard, and after traveling extensively during his junior year, he found the earth to be his campus. One of his first jobs was Managing Editor of *WorldPaper*, a monthly publication in five languages with a circulation of more than one million.

Mr. Gerzon is an author, mediator, and leadership consultant. For more than twenty years, he has been president of the Mediators Foundation, with a special interest in global leadership. In the late 1990s, he was chosen to design and facilitate the U.S. House of Representatives' Bipartisan Congressional Retreat, and he continues to conduct dialogue trainings for various U.S. government offices.

Mr. Gerzon is also founder and co-chair of the Global Leadership Network, a group of leadership experts and practitioners from throughout the world who are developing a book, a workshop, and an educational curriculum.

About the Contributors

Neville Isdell is Chairman and Chief Executive Officer of The Coca-Cola Company, maker of one of the world's leading soft drinks and other beverages.

In 1966 Mr. Isdell joined The Coca-Cola Company at a local bottling company in Zambia. From then until 1989, he held a variety of positions and was Senior Vice President of the Company from January 1989 to February 1998. He also served as president of the Greater Europe Group from January 1995 to February 1998.

Mr. Isdell has also been chairman and CEO of Coca-Cola Beverages Plc, from July 1998 to September 2000. He was CEO of Coca-Cola Hellenic Bottling Company S.A. from September 2000 to May 2001 and vice chairman from May 2001 to December 2001. From January 2002 to May 2004, Mr. Isdell was an international consultant to the Company.

Mr. Isdell has been Chairman of the Board and CEO of the highly recognizable Coca-Cola Company since June 2004.

He is also a director of SunTrust Banks, Inc., a position he has held since December 2004.

Robert Johnson is the founder of Black Entertainment Television, a leading cable network targeted toward African American subscribers.

During his early career, Mr. Johnson worked for the Corporation for Public Broadcasting and the National Urban League's Washington, D.C., office. He also worked as press secretary for Walter Fauntroy, the congressional delegate from Washington, D.C.

About the Contributors

In 1976 Mr. Johnson became Vice President of Government Relations for the National Cable & Telecommunications Association. He left this position in 1979 to start Black Entertainment Television, which began broadcasting in January 1980.

In 1991 the company went public, but in 1998, Mr. Johnson took the company private once more, before selling the company to Viacom in 1999. Mr. Johnson stayed on as chairman and CEO until 2005.

Mr. Johnson is founder, chairman, and CEO of The RLJ Companies, a business network that provides strategic investment and direction in and for the financial services, real estate, hospitality/restaurant, professional sports, film production, gaming, and recording industries.

In addition, Mr. Johnson serves on the following boards of directors: NBA Board of Governors, Lowe's Companies Inc., International Management Group (IMG), American Film Institute, Strayer Education, Inc., Johns Hopkins University, The Business Council, Wal-Mart Advisory Council, and Deutsche Bank Advisory Board. He is a former director of Hilton Hotels Corporation (1994–2006).

Kay Koplovitz is the founder of Koplovitz & Co., a media and investment advisory firm. Ms. Koplovitz is also the founder of USA Networks, a leading cable network.

Ms. Koplovitz became the first woman network president in television history when she founded USA Networks in 1977 under the banner of Madison

Square Garden Sports. It was the first advertising-supported basic cable network. She is also a former CEO and Chairman of USA Networks.

As a visionary of what sports television would become, Ms. Koplovitz launched major professional and collegiate sports on cable television by negotiating the first contracts for Major League Baseball, the National Basketball Association, and the National Hockey League.

In 1992 Ms. Koplovitz was instrumental in the launch of the Sci-Fi Channel. Two years later she launched USA Networks International. She subsequently launched Springboard, a nonprofit forum to connect women with venture capital.

Currently, Ms. Koplovitz is the founder and principal of Koplovitz & Co., a leading media advisory and investment firm that specializes in marketing and growth strategies.

Ms. Koplovitz is also chairman of Liz Claiborne Inc., and vice chairperson of Sun New Media. She was formerly on the board of Instinet.

Sir Peter Middleton is the former chairman of Barclays Group, one of the top corporate banking providers, and the current chairman of Camelot Group plc, the licensed operator for the UK National Lottery.

Sir Peter enjoyed a long and distinguished career in HM Treasury spanning thirty years, ultimately ascending to become Permanent Secretary from 1983 to 1991. He spent the next thirteen years with Barclays as group deputy chairman and executive

chairman of its investment bank, BZW. In 1997 he
became chairman of Barclays Capital.

In May 1998 he relinquished his executive responsibilities but remained a nonexecutive director
of Barclays and Barclays Bank. Later that year, he
resumed the helm following the unexpected resig-
nation of the chief executive.

Sir Peter was then appointed group chairman in
April 1999, and in October stepped down as group
chief executive. He left Barclays in late 2004. He
took on the chairmanship of Camelot, the operator
of The National Lottery, in September 2004.

He is also deputy chairman and independent
director of United Utilities, and is on the board of
the National Institute of Economic and Social
Research.

Barbara Stocking is the director general of Oxfam,
an organization working to overcome poverty and
suffering around the world.

Ms. Stocking is a former member of the top
management team of the National Health Service
(NHS). In her eight years there, she worked as
regional director, and more recently she served as
director of the Modernization Agency, charged
with modernizing the NHS.

She has broad experience of healthcare systems,
policy, and practice, including periods at the World
Health Organization in West Africa and the National Academy of Sciences in the United States.

Ms. Stocking joined Oxfam GB as Director in
May 2001. Her interests have been in bringing

About the Contributors

about change and development in healthcare. This is something she has brought to Oxfam GB's work in fighting poverty through humanitarian relief, development work, and advocacy.

Robert Sutton is a professor of Management Science and Engineering at Stanford University. At Stanford he co-leads the Center for Work, Technology, and Organization; and is a faculty member in the Stanford Technology Ventures Program.

A former professor of Haas Business School, he has been at Stanford since joining in 1983 after completing his PhD at the University of Michigan. Over the last twenty years, he has been developing the simple core message that long-term performance is dependent on having a number of good ideas that are subsequently implemented.

A prolific writer, Professor Sutton has authored *The Knowing-Doing Gap* and *Hard Facts, Dangerous Half-Truths, and Total Nonsense: Profiting from Evidence-Based Management* (both co-authored with Jeffrey Pfeffer) and *Weird Ideas That Work*.

Professor Sutton teaches in Stanford's professional education program. He also consults with a number of global blue-chip companies, including Ernst & Young, The Gap, Hewlett-Packard, IBM, McDonald's, PepsiCo, Procter & Gamble, and Xerox.

He has been a fellow of the Center for Advanced Study in the Behavioral Sciences in 1986–1987, 1994–1995, and 2002–2003.

About the Contributors

William Ury is the coauthor of the best-selling book *Getting to Yes.*

Mr. Ury earned his BA from Yale and his PhD, in social anthropology, from Harvard. He has conducted research in corporate boardrooms and other locations throughout the world.

Mr. Ury is the cofounder of Harvard Law School's Program on Negotiation and is the Director of the Global Negotiation Project. As one of the world's foremost experts in negotiation, he has mediated everything from corporate mergers to sensitive political issues. Mr. Ury also cofounded the International Negotiation Network, which is chaired by President Jimmy Carter, and he remains an adviser.

Mr. Ury's clients include AT&T, IBM, Ford Motor Company, the Pentagon, and the U.S. State Department. He is also the author of *Getting Past No.*

Sir Mark Weinberg is Cofounder and President of St. James's Place Capital plc, a leader in wealth management services. He has more than forty years' experience in the financial services market.

In 1961 he founded Abbey Life Assurance Company, where he formed one of the UK's first property funds. Ten years later, he started Hambro Life Assurance (now part of Zurich Financial Services), which grew to become the largest unit-linked life assurance company in the United Kingdom. There he formed the first retail managed fund.

Sir Mark was deputy chairman of the Securities and Investment Board—the principal U.K. regulatory body—from its inception in 1985 until 1990.

About the Contributors

In 1991, he cofounded St. James's Place Capital plc, the wealth management group of which he remains president.

Gary Wilson is Chairman of Northwest Airlines, one of the world's largest airlines.

Mr. Wilson served for eleven years in various executive positions at Marriott Corporation. As executive vice president and chief financial officer, he was responsible for strategic planning, financial management and corporate development, and had operating responsibility for Marriott's In-Flight Catering Division.

In 1985, Mr. Wilson joined The Walt Disney Company as executive vice president, chief financial officer, and director. He served as chief financial officer until 1990, and he resigned from the board in July 2006.

In 1989 Mr. Wilson joined Northwest Airlines. From April 1991 to 1997 he was co-chairman of the Board of Directors, and in April 1997 he became Chairman.

Mr. Wilson is also a director of Yahoo! Inc., a position he has held since November 2001, and a director of CB Richard Ellis Group, Inc., since September 2001.

⊰ ACKNOWLEDGMENTS ⊱

First and foremost, a heartfelt thanks goes to all of the executives who have shared their hard-earned experience and battle-tested insights for the Lessons Learned series.

Angelia Herrin, at Harvard Business School Publishing, consistently offered unwavering support, good humor, and counsel from the inception of this ambitious project.

Julia Ely, Hollis Heimbouch, and David Goehring provided invaluable editorial direction, perspective, and encouragement. Much appreciation goes to Jennifer Lynn for her research and diligent attention to detail. Many thanks to the entire HBSP team of designers, copy editors, and marketing professionals who helped bring this series to life.

Finally, thanks to our fellow cofounder James MacKinnon and the entire Fifty

Acknowledgments

Lessons team for the tremendous amount of time, effort, and steadfast support for this project.

—Adam Sodowick
Andy Hasoon
Directors and Cofounders
Fifty Lessons